BE A
MASTER™
OF
SUCCESS

DR. KOUSOULI'S *33* MASTER
SECRETS TO ACHIEVING
YOUR DREAMS

Dr. Theodoros Kousouli

A Personal Empowerment Book

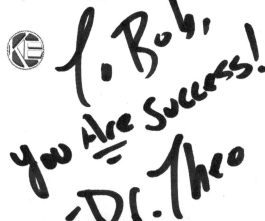

T. Bob,
you Are Success!
-Dr. Theo

The BE A MASTER™ BOOK SERIES (http://www.BEAMASTER.com) trademarked brand and work is Copyright of Dr. Theodoros Kousouli.

The KOUSOULI® mark and the Kousouli® Method 4R Intervention health system are registered trademarks of Theodoros D. Kousouli D.C., CHt. and Kousouli Enterprises.

Heartfelt gratitude to the following for their contributions:
Editing & research assistance: Latasha Doyle
Layout coordinator: Gustavo Martinez
Cover photography: Matthew A. Cooke

ISBN: 978-0997328592   Softcover
ISBN: 978-0997627602   Epub
ISBN: 978-0997627619   Kindle

Library of Congress Control Number: 2016909171

Kousouli Enterprises
Printed in the United States of America

CONTENTS

DISCLAIMER

In a land where being politically correct seems more 'right' than standing for the 'truth,' or more desired than expressing an honest opinion, it's sad that I must digress and add the following legal disclaimer to remind you, the reader, that *you must think for yourself.*

The writings in this book are based on my personal research, experience, interpretations, and beliefs. Your personal beliefs will affect your ability to review this material, as you will put it through your own filters. I intend to help you break through your pre-programming for success, and this book is a guide for you to grow. But it is not by any means the final word on the subject. Although the contents herein have worked for my definition of success, they are not by any means a guarantee that they will work for you, and may work differently based on your individual circumstances and application of the material discussed. Only you can guarantee your own success.

I encourage you, the reader, to research, analyze, and develop your own opinions on the subject matters discussed. As a holistic health care provider, I express the truth as I have come to know it. It is my duty to aid in the growth of my beloved patients, family, and friends with this love so they too may reach the heights of what their Creator made possible for them to be.

Theodoros Kousouli D.C., CHt.

LEGAL DISCLAIMER

This book is dedicated to the men in my life who showed me how to not only work hard and smart, but most importantly - correctly. Much love to my father, who showed me what dedication and strong work ethic looks like; my uncle Tony who showed me how to make work a playful activity; my Uncle Nick, who showed me to be the best in my craft; and my early healing mentors, Dr. Kostas, Dr. Lewis, and Dr. Khalsa, whom I watched serve the public with love, creating miracles with their bare hands.

"I'm a success today because I had a friend who believed in me, and I didn't have the heart to let him down."

~ Abraham Lincoln

Introduction

The year was 1995 in a tiny south Jersey town no one has ever heard
of. I was in cap and gown, holding my first diploma and graduating
high school. The Spartan was our mascot, and I felt like I was an
actual Spartan, not only by ancestry but also by deed. I was going to
go out there and conquer new lands, spread my wings, and forge my
way by becoming something useful in society. My big journey was
about to begin. While it seemed at that time like it would take me
eons to reach my goals, just a blink of an eye later - I was an author,
speaker, and doctor in Beverly Hills, CA. What!? How did that happen!? How in the world did I go from a small town that wasn't even
on the map to being a highly sought-after successful healer, helping
people change their lives through mind-body advancement in one of
the most luxurious towns in America? Was it luck, the right place at
the right time, or was I just special somehow?

Well, we all like to think we are special don't we? Yes, we all are
special - in our unique way. But I had to really get over some of my
early limiting beliefs and life challenges and look deep within in order to really bring out the best in myself. Once I did, I was able to
piece together the clues that made the difference. I've contemplated
this so much over the years, and combined it with the experiences
of others who rose up along with me. What I have found is that by
applying certain core principles into my life - and sticking to them

- the small steps lead to giant leaps. You can do this also; it's entirely possible – no matter what your current situation is. It just takes a shift in perspective and application of set ideas. It is with great pleasure I bestow this information to you for your ascension and success. Apply this wisdom into your life and your business, and you may also gain the lift you're seeking in life.

In This Book, You Will Learn Success Secrets That Will Help You:

✓ Understand how today's world is controlled through mass hypnosis. You will learn how this affects *you* in your life and business, and you will gain the tools to break free from others' control in order to create your own success. It's time to be a shepherd, not a sheep.

✓ Understand and define: covert hypnosis; the conscious, subconscious, and superconscious (higher) mind; and ego. You will learn how hypnosis bypasses the rational thinking brain and programs the subconscious. You'll be given the tools you need to overcome this programming, and return the power to your own mind.

✓ Look into your inner self, and embrace your special gifts. In this book, you will learn the importance of using regression hypnotherapy to heal one's prior past/trauma, remove phobias, break bad habits, and support self-Improvement. Investing and learning about yourself are the two most powerful things you can do to be successful in this life.

✓ Build a strong, solid "Why I do." This is why you wake up in the morning – every morning – and strive to live the life you love. In this book, you will learn how important your passions and excitement are in breaking yourself free from the herd.

✓ Re-program your mind into positive autopilot. This book will help you by showing you how to remove old thoughts, habits, and relationships that don't serve you any longer. You will re-train that voice in your head and change the course of your life.

✓ Reconsider your core "power" group by finding a better set of network counterparts who have the same mindset as you. This book will illustrate the importance of "Like attracts like" in regards to business and connections.

✓ Encourage yourself and other go-getters, business leaders, VIPS, CEOs, or like-minded people who want to step out and lead with more confidence. You need other people to succeed with you, and this book will show you how to honor relationships that empower you and others.

✓ Know how to push through and believe in yourself even during the hard times. This book will help you overcome your fears of failure, and inspire you to finally get excited about your talents and creations.

You are here to create, not to be a follower of someone else's creation. This book will teach you what you need to know about breaking through your preprogrammed negative thinking, and become who you truly are meant to be. Success is a mindset. Get ready!

Chapter One:
Brainwashed into Ignorance

"The secret of freedom lies in educating people, whereas the
secret of tyranny is in keeping them ignorant."
~ *Maximilien Robespierre*

You **are being hypnotized every day.** The society we live in operates under the perception that what we are told via television, advertisements, social media, and every other input is *the whole truth*. What many of us never take the time to understand is that this is a form of hypnotism.

Hypnotism doesn't just happen in a quiet room with a swinging pocket watch ticking back and forth in front of your face. We do not need a controlled setting to initiate a hypnotic sequence. Hypnotism is simply the ability to trigger focus and lack of external awareness; essentially, hypnotism is increasing your suggestibility. Think about the last time you were absolutely sucked into a news broadcast and didn't hear your spouse talking to you, or when you were reading a textbook so intently that you didn't notice your surroundings. That is a hypnotic state; really, it's that simple.

Sources of Thought Control

You probably think thought control and hypnotism only occur under the influence of some evil villain with magical hypnotic abilities. Sadly for all of us, this is just not the truth. Hypnosis is a tool, by itself neutral – it is not evil or good – but can be used for either, depending on the intent by its user. As water is good if we drink it to sustain life, and considered bad if we drown in it to end life; the intent of how you use something is everything. There are people, companies, and entire societies that want to use hypnosis for dishonorable reasons.

It's not hard to do, either, because humans are wired for a certain amount of suggestibility, especially as children. Thought control is everywhere in our society, even infiltrating areas you consider "safe."

- **Education.** Until the brain is fully formed around the age of 21, humans are like a sponge – we soak up new knowledge easily. What we can't do, until our brain is fully formed, is differentiate between good and bad information. Often, we take what we hear enough at face value. This is why our education system is such a huge source of thought control. Consider how many history books leave out parts that make the U.S. look bad, or how only Creation and abstinence are taught in some areas. What a child isn't exposed to can't be a threat. In school you are taught to regurgitate what you learn to get the grade. Seldom, if ever, are students encouraged to think for themselves and challenge the teacher.

- **Politics.** If you live in the United States, odds are you're either Republican or Democrat. You probably hold very strong opinions, and probably believe that people on the other side of the fence are brainwashed or just plain stupid. Consider where you get your information – most likely from large media outlets – and consider what they have to gain from your support rather than your vote. Also consider this: Where are the 'candidates' leading you to? To more abundance and prosperity, or to more of the same pain and misery? When you look closer at the system, you will awaken to the fact that both sides are controlled by the same force, and your time and energy would be better spent on developing yourself; not buying into the political spin.

- **Religion.** Have you ever wondered how so many people could believe in something so *obviously* fake? Cults and violent religious sects tend to get disgusted glances and many wonder just what in the world is wrong with them. How could they ever believe as they do? Consider the power that leaders in these religions/groups have - that is hypnosis and thought control at its finest. Also take a moment to consider your own beliefs, and the people you follow without question.

- **The 'Authorities.'** In our world, we look to those with expertise, authority, and power to tell us what to do. The Centers for Disease Control tell us about Ebola, Bird Flu, and Zika virus. We hear about their supposed spread rates, everyone buys mosquito repellant, freaks out, and stops traveling. The White House is raising the terror alert; everyone panics. The American Medical Association backs a new drug for cholesterol; everyone asks their doctors for a prescription. A new study shows that eye twitching is actually a new mental illness; everyone asks for a diagnosis. Because these institutions are considered an authority, we comply with their obviously superior knowledge, and we never question or challenge their 'authority.'

Thought control is everywhere. We are easily swayed, and we have so many external sources that influence how we will live our lives. But we are willingly exposing ourselves to insane levels of hypnosis on a daily basis – not including the sources listed above. The single greatest source of thought control and hypnotism comes from technology; our Internet, handheld smartphones, wrist devices, and our televisions.

Statistics That Will Shock You

> *"Hundreds of billions of dollars are spent every year*
> *to control the public mind."*
> ~ Noam Chomsky

For many people, the idea that they are being hypnotized and brain-washed is too bitter a pill to swallow. Some even consider it a ridiculous conspiracy theory with no support whatsoever. But take a look at these statistics, and decide for yourself:

- 90% of all media is owned by "The Big Six" – GE, News-Corp, Disney, Viacom, Time Warner, and CBS. According to a *Business Insider* article published in 2012, the Big Six control:

  o 70% of all cable broadcasts
  o The three most read newspapers in the world (*Wall Street Journal, The Sun,* and *The Australian*)
  o 80% of all radio broadcasts
  o 50% of all movie productions

- Adults are exposed to over *590* minutes worth of ads and other media *in a single day*! That's almost 10 hours of passive and active media and marketing exposure a day (from TV, radio, Internet, ads, etc.), according to Media Dynamics, Inc.

- ABC News ran a piece in 2007, stating that nearly $20 billion is used to target children and teens in ads. Marketing statistics show that children have over 90% influence on purchases made in the house, making them the weakest link and the best bet for advertisers.

- Audi, MTV, Nabisco, Verizon, and many other huge companies use hypnotism in their focus groups to understand consumer thought processes and memories attached to specific products. They find trigger words, images, and experiences that mass-influence people in a group hypnotic state, according to Beth Synyder-Bulik, a reporter at *Advertising Age*. They then replicate these hypnotic states in their ads.

• Nobody that is under a hypnotic spell realizes they're being hypnotized. Nobody. This is called covert hypnosis, or "hidden hypnosis." Advertisers know how to implant commands and messages that bypass your thinking, rational, conscious mind. It's true that you can only be hypnotized if you give your full permission, but you passively give your permission when you give something your attention. Simply being present and focused on something is giving your mind's energy to it, like watching television or a movie. You "check out" and you get really deep into it. Wherever you focus your attention, you are giving permission to be influenced by that material – whether it's good or bad.

TV, ads, subliminal messages – these are all very real threats to your individuality and your success. In addition, they waste your time and add no value to your core life mission. The thing about being hypnotized is that you *don't know that you're hypnotized*. What I want to do is wake you up so you can erase the hardwired programming in your mind in order to regain your personal power.

If you're interested in learning more about the exact mechanism of hypnotism and how those "in power" use hypnotism and thought control, check out my other book, *BE A MASTER™ OF PSYCHIC ENERGY, or attend one of my powerful seminars for live teaching instruction.*

A Hypnotized Society

Listen to the inner monologue you have running through your brain on any given day. Odds are, it sounds something like this:

> *"Must buy that, must do that activity, must say this, must not say that... I can't do that, I have to do this instead... I shouldn't do that... There's no way that will work... That's too risky."*

We have a constant stream of thought and inner monologue running through our brains every day. We listen to that voice in our head because "we think" that it's *us*; you can't ignore yourself! And what happens when that voice believes everything external influences say? You believe the limiting statements, you follow the crowd, and you don't try to test the limits. You don't try to reach your full potential because you're confused, wondering if what you are hearing in your head is your own thoughts, or beliefs that others have force-fed you.

Even worse, everyone around you believes their inner voice, too- and their inner voice believes everything *it* hears! Can't get a song or commercial you heard this morning on the radio out of your head? Can't help but always feel anxious, worried, or negative for no reason and you don't know why? We live in a culture where we believe what has always been told to us - by our parents, teachers, grandparents, and preachers - and we also internalize the hypnotic messages we receive from TV, ads, social media, and "thought influencers" in general. Once thought patterns are repeated in the conscious mind frequently enough, they pass into the subconscious mind and, like a virus, they replicate by implanting into the automatic subconscious mind. Our egos, which are there to protect and help us navigate our world safely, can easily get out of control when under this influence. Our egos start sending us into a materialistic, super-hoarding overdrive, which we may start to define ourselves with.

We believe we need that house, that car, that bag of money in the bank. But we also believe that to get that level of success, we have to take the "tried and true" path, we can't take risks; what if we lose everything!? We believe that buying that thing we saw on that commercial will bring happiness, or that following the safe path will give us the rewards we seek. Every time we try to explore a different path - maybe starting a business, starting that creative hobby, dropping everything to travel the world – the world seems to rear up and say, **"What are you doing? You can't do that."** And so you fall back in line, one of the sheep once again.

Social pressure to conform makes us afraid to expand our horizons, and what influences society? Ideas drilled into us; from birth, from the media, and from technology. Consider the scare tactics on the news: don't travel to the Middle East or you'll be taken prisoner. Don't start that business right now, the economy is going to tank again! And then we are repeatedly exposed to the horror stories, the failures, and the people who thought they were different, falling back to the "real world." We are told that true successes are flukes, or a product of dumb luck. You can't replicate those results; **Who do you think you are?** We are given specific limits to our potential, and we are told that *this* is our place in the world.

But I have great news for you: **Your full potential is greater than what you've been brainwashed into believing is possible. You are greater than you have been conditioned to believe. You can learn the system you are living in, work the system in your own unique way, and BE A MASTER™ of the system so you can generate your personal power like never before. That's how you become a success and manifest your dreams into reality. Let's get to work!**

Chapter Two:
Put Yourself on Positive Autopilot

We have been programmed our entire lives to believe as everyone else in society does. We grow up thinking we need to live a certain way, make a certain amount of money, or have a family that fits a specific mold. This constant barrage of limiting beliefs does exactly what it's designed to do: Keep us in line. The previous chapter detailed the exact ways we're being controlled; ways you probably never even thought of. As they say, "Ignorance is bliss." But now that you know how you may have been negatively hypnotized, what are you going to do with that information, and how will you reboot your mind?

Hypnotize Yourself for Success

I'm here to tell you that you can reroute your programming, and you can **hypnotize yourself for success**. You don't have to live with limiting beliefs, and you can quiet that inner monologue that says, "No, you can't/shouldn't/won't." Just as you've been controlled into *believing* you can't, you can reprogram your brain to *know* that you can.

But how? You start with deleting the old voices, creating a new, positive inner monologue, and overwriting the pre-programmed negativity. If, in your life, you've felt like you have been floating helplessly in the ocean without a sailboat, know that you're not alone. But while others row past you without throwing you a life vest, you now realize it's time to get into your own canoe and row until your canoe becomes a yacht. Eventually, you'll be commanding the high seas of life in a high-powered ocean liner. Take action!

The next 10 chapters will give you action steps to programming that positive autopilot in your life.

Action Steps for Setting Your Autopilot to Positive

You *can* train your mind on a subconscious level. I teach my students to catch themselves every time they negatively speak against themselves or others. Once they master the process of catching themselves, the next step is to analyze why they said or thought something so negative. If it comes out of their mouth, it's more destructive than just a thought, and must be neutralized by positive self-talk. Once you catch yourself thinking or saying something negative, immediately counter it with a positive thought on the same person or subject.

For instance, if you have a negative thought when you glance over at someone less fortunate than you, counter the negative thought or feeling with a positive remark or trait you like about the person. This neutralizes the mind and allows for positive creation. Then, think and verbally say something positive, and follow up with yet another positive idea. The next step I recommend is to record yourself talking in a positive manner. Use your phone for recording, download a free recorder app, or buy a digital recorder if you like. Record yourself for fifteen minutes, talking to yourself as if you were your most positive cheerleader, being sure to point out your best features and the many things you love about yourself. You can repeat things as many times as you need, and ramble on as you wish. Be sure to tell yourself what goals you will accomplish, amazing feats you will overcome, and what you will attain. You know this because you do deserve it all.

Tell yourself how attractive you are, how talented you are, how special you are, how successful you are, and how much you love yourself. After fifteen minutes of recording time, save the file. If you wish to add relaxing meditation music to it you may, but be sure not to drown out your voice with music. Now, here's the magic; instead of listening to worthless radio top ten playlists, play your positive self-talk file every night to yourself as you drift off to sleep. Your subconscious will pick up directions from your own voice; you will rewrite your subconscious mind's programming and get a huge boost where it counts - your life!

You may also check out my website, www.DrKousouli.com, for more powerful hypnosis training products to help you gain an edge for success!

Chapter Three:
Build Your "Why I Do"

O ne of the best things you can do for yourself is question your existing beliefs. Whenever you think, "I have to do x, y, or z," stop and take a minute to simply ask yourself, "Why?" Most of what we have been taught and what society has drilled into our heads doesn't have a rhyme or reason. We do it because "that's just what people always did before." In order to overcome this programming and put ourselves on positive autopilot, we really need to redefine and build our "why."

Dr. Kousouli's Success Secret Tip #1
BUILD AN UNBELIEVABLE 'WHY I DO'

"The starting point of all achievement is DESIRE. Keep this constantly in mind. Weak desire brings weak results, just as a small fire makes a small amount of heat."
~ Napoleon Hill

Our "Why I Do" applies to everything we do in life, even though most people assume that it counts only for business and career success. What I've learned through the years is that defining the "why" for nearly every action we take can help us become more genuine, true versions of ourselves. By defining the "why" in every aspect of our life, we are free to create with clarity; we know why we are here, and we move towards making that "why" a reality, hour after hour and day after day.

Of course, this is not just a simple activity; it takes time, it takes commitment, and it takes guts. It's scary to wake up every morning and do what you love because your life isn't going to look like the rest of the world's. Even scarier, the life you're aiming for looks much more exciting and drastically different than the one you're currently living. This is a scary thought for most people. They'd rather stay within their safe comfort zones than to go for a better version of life. They don't feel they deserve better and think that where they are is "enough" for right now. This is crazy!

Why "Why I Do" Works

We are beings of instant gratification who seek pleasure; our brain is wired to attract pleasure and avoid pain. We can use this knowledge to our advantage, though, when creating our "Why I do." If your "Why I do" is connected to pleasure in your brain, you're more likely to get up and do what you need to do with passion. From a hypnosis stand point, the best way to create a hypnotic trance is to connect a specific stimuli with a cue (in this case, a positive feeling – a "Why I do"). Connecting pleasure and what you need to do will make sure it really "sticks."

To illustrate this point: Tim dislikes the stinky smell in the garage on trash night, as the smell seeps into the den. Tim loves a fresh, clean garage and den that both smell like lavender. Tim reasons with himself that if he takes out the trash he can spray and enjoy his favorite organic lavender scented sprays he purchased from his therapist's office. He decides to look forward to the positive scent of the lavender in the air, and the trash chore is now looked forward to with joy, rather than with dread.

More Pleasure, More Positivity, More Passion

Spiritual satisfaction, community connections, providing for your family, etc., are all valid reasons to get up in the morning. When you connect your passion in business to your "Why I do," you're making it easier for yourself to get up in the morning and easier for you to stay the course - even when things get rough. But saying, "I want to make a lot of money" is a weak "Why I do." Why? Because paper and credit money only keep you motivated for so long. What happens when you've "made enough" or when you think, "It's not worth the money today"?

Create "Why's" that don't waver, and that will motivate you each and every day to keep moving. The more sources of pleasure you can create for your "Why I do," the stronger your positive autopilot.

Action Steps for Creating Your "Why I Do"

1. Get out a pen and paper.

2. List all of the things that make you get up in the morning, in order of what makes you feel the happiest/strongest. For example, this could be your children, your clients, your excitement to achieve your goals. If you write down money, consider: What could the money offer in terms of freedom or fun?

3. Keep this list, or write a nice, neat one. Tape or prop up the list next to your bed, mirror in the bathroom, desk, or anywhere you'll see it every day. Read *BE A MASTER™ OF PSYCHIC ENERGY* to learn more about how to use this list along with an "In-Vision" board to keep you pumped up!

4. Whenever you start to wander back to your pre-programmed, negative autopilot, look at this list and remember "Why I Do."

Chapter Four:
Don't Be Like the Rest of Them – There is Only One *You*

We are taught from a young age to blend in so we can be loved; you don't want to be at the bottom of the class, but you don't want to be at the top either. Buy the same clothes as everyone so you can fit in. "Don't be such a nerd, don't dress too crazy, don't do x/y/z." But the reality is: There is only one you, and you were put on this earth for a reason. It's time to honor that reason, and start creating like the Creator intended you to.

Dr. Kousouli's Success Secret Tip #2
DON'T LET OTHERS TELL YOU HOW TO LIVE LIFE–ESPECIALLY YOURS

"Your time is limited, so don't waste it living someone else's life."
~ *Steve Jobs*

Do you remember how frustrated you used to get when your parents or family members would try to project their hopes and dreams on to you? As a teenager, didn't you just rail against the, "I just want what's best for you," lecture your family spouted?

And yet, as adults, the majority of us let other people and hidden media messages control our lives. We let commercials tell us what products to buy, we let the Joneses next door tell us we're not doing enough, and we let social media make us feel like we just aren't good enough.

If you didn't want to listen to your parents (who genuinely do try to have your best interests at heart), why would you take the advice of someone or some*thing* that definitely doesn't have your interests in mind? It is great when someone can offer constructive criticism that you can use, but **start thinking for yourself,** and start questioning anyone or anything that tries to tell you how to live your life. **Research everything and make educated choices only after you're satisfied with all the data. Be especially wary of T.V. commercials, religious groups, magazines, documentaries, and political ads that want to sway your mind - usually away from what is naturally best for you.**

Dr. Kousouli's Success Secret Tip #3
NO ONE IS YOUR COMPETITION BUT YOU

"There is nothing noble in being superior to your fellow man; true nobility is being superior to your former self."
~ Ernest Hemingway

In the same vein, many of us feel the need to "succeed" in life merely to prove to others that we've "made it" or that we worked hard enough to get to x amount of money, possessions, experiences, etc. But that's putting all the power in *their* hands, not yours. Why do you need to prove to anyone that you're happy, you're successful, you're growing? Do you really have to put yourself in financial debt, working harder to pay banks a monthly fee in order to "show off" that new car?

How many times have you compared yourself to others? Whether in life; "They have a better house, sexier spouse, cuter kids, etc.," or in your career; "They have the practice/position/salary/prestige that I want." Instead of thinking about what we can do to be on their level, we think about all the things they have that we don't. And again – we assign these things to fate.

"They just got lucky," or, "I can't be successful now because they've already done it." I have news for you: There is enough room for everyone at the top. Just because someone did or is doing the exact same thing you want to do doesn't mean you can't keep going and do it better or differently. You present an entirely unique perspective to whatever it is you're passionate about. Those people are not your competition – **you are.**

Every day, we need to compete against ourselves in order to constantly improve who we are and what we can provide to the world with our talents. When you let that pre-programmed inner voice tell you, "It's too late," or, "Someone else is already doing what you wanted to do," you're not growing. That's exactly where the media and sources of hypnosis want you to be - stagnant. "Don't progress, Don't grow, Listen to us, We know better." By recognizing these negative programmed thoughts, you can fight them and finally realize that the only way to become what you want to be or get where you want to go is to **constantly grow and challenge yourself on your own terms.**

Work on challenging yourself for your own personal reasons, and stop looking to external influences to affect your behavior. Don't work harder so you can show the Joneses who is boss – work so you can have a better life and be happy with what you're doing. Create only the way you can create, and challenge yourself to create more and create differently every. single. day.

Dr. Kousouli's Success Secret Tip #4
FIND NEW WAYS TO DO OLD THINGS

"Often, finding meaning is not about doing things differently; it is about seeing familiar things in new ways."
~ Rachel Naomi Remen

The one truth I hold most dear in this life is that we were all put on Earth to create; our duty in life is to create whatever it is we are gifted with. For me, that gift is leading my fellow mankind to healing. For you, that gift may be making beautiful music, raising healthy, well-adjusted children, rocking the stock market, becoming an exceptional actor, model, comedian, etc. You're creating something with your gift, and that is your one true purpose in life – to find, cultivate, nurture, and express your talent for the betterment and enjoyment of all.

In order to break our social bonds and our collective hypnotism, we have to be willing to learn new methods and approach life with a fresh perspective. Obviously, the "same-old-same-old" isn't getting us anywhere. In order to truly separate ourselves from the herd, we have to create with our gifts in new ways. Think of how many entertainers, such as magicians and illusionists, have recreated themselves in the years since Houdini. Or how many comedians have reinvented the art of the laugh through their own version of comedy since the times of Charlie Chaplin. There is definitely not only one way to make people laugh!

We can't expect to find success in the same paths our fathers and grandfathers did, and we can't use our talents in the same ways as those who came before us. We have to think, act, play, work, and *be* different in order to grow spiritually, physically, emotionally, and socially. Remember that the people who do not grow, who do not change, will stagnate – and that is the opposite of creation. That is an insult to the Creator, and it means we are denying our reason for existing.

Dr. Kousouli's Success Secret Tip #5
EAT LOTS OF HUMBLE PIE

"The humble man makes room for progress; the proud man believes he is already there."
~ Ed Parker

It's natural, when we gain a modicum of "success" as society defines it, to start to feel a little proud of ourselves. Take note: there is a difference in pride and ego. Pride says, "Yes I can, and yes I will," while ego says, "Of course I can, I can do anything without fail." Be proud and celebrate your victories, but do not let your ego take the credit or speak for you. Remember, there will always be someone happier, younger, or more successful than you at any given time, so stay humble.

You want to set yourself apart from the "successful crowd" in this manner. It's so important to stomp down your ego if it starts to rear its deceptively inconspicuous head. One way to do this: listen, don't talk. Listen to people who are different than you, who have more experience than you, who have something to say that you may-be don't want to hear. If you want to be different, you have to think differently, and to think differently, you need to have different values and influencers in your life.

Dr. Kousouli's Success Secret Tip #6
DON'T HATE THE HATERS

"The art of knowing is knowing what to ignore."
~ Rumi

One thing you will notice when you start to reprogram yourself and put more emphasis on your positive autopilot is that people will start trying to drag you down. They may make small comments that make you doubt yourself, like, "Oh, I really hope you can do this because it would really suck if everything fell through." Or, "I used to think I could do that, too, until I grew up and had responsibilities."

These people are usually ones we thought were friends, but it can also be subconscious negative hypnosis from society at large. Start-ing that new business? You'll inevitably hear about the economy and how hard it is to start a business in this climate on the news. About to go back to school? You'll hear all about how hard it is to teach an old dog new tricks. **Whatever it is that you want to do, do not listen to the negativity that will flock to you. You will be challenged every time you are about to graduate to a new level.**

Negativity Will Seek You Out

Negative energy seeks to quench positive energy. If you know anything about the Periodic Table of Elements, you know that atoms with a negative energy seek to bond with atoms that have positive energy. The same goes for humans; negative energy seeks to gain from positive energy every time.

Unlike atoms, though, we can control our environments and those who gain access to our energy. For this reason, surround yourself with people who are positive, and provide *constructive criticism* and useful feedback. You don't want people who are there to tear you down, only people who will build you up. And you don't want to drag down your energy trying to get back at the haters; don't hate the haters, and don't play their game!

Dr. Kousouli's Success Secret Tip #7
AIM RIDICULOUSLY HIGH, AND DON'T EVER SETTLE

"All who invest in refining their mind have already aimed ridiculously high, for most of society strives for the pinnacle of mediocrity."
~ Dr. Theo Kousouli

Why be/have/do less in life than you know you are worth? What sets you apart more than aiming for the stars when everyone else is perfectly fine with staying on the ground? Even though life, society, and even those closest to you are bound to tell you that your dreams are too big, the true creators among us will try anyways; and if we fail, we will try and try again.

Think of being uniquely different as being "improved," despite what our society has drilled into our heads from birth about "fitting in." Don't be hypnotized into thinking only one way; stand out and create success based on what makes you *you*, rather than what everyone else tells you your success should look like.

Action Steps for Setting Yourself Apart

1. Take out pen and paper.

2. Write down your strengths and weaknesses in business, relationships, and general attitudes. But do it with a twist – only write down what traits you have that you notice nobody else does. Don't write down "I'm a hard worker" unless you have an instance where that has set you apart from the crowd. For weaknesses, it might be something like, "I care about my clients more than other businesses do."

3. Read this list, making sure that you've given a "What makes me stand out" statement with each one. Review it, and use those differences to help you develop a sense of who you are and what you contribute.

4. Then, list all your ridiculously high goals you wish to achieve. How does the previous list about how you're different help the list of ridiculously high goals? How can each trait you listed contribute to your success?

Chapter Five:
For Mo' Money, Follow Your Passion - Not the Dollar Signs

One of the biggest lies we are told as human beings, especially in Western culture, is that our worth is defined by the amount of money we make. Think about how many times, as a child, someone asked you what you wanted to be when you grew up. Maybe you said, "I want to be an astronaut/lawyer/doctor," and the person said, "That's a great idea; you'll be rich!" Or maybe you said, "I want to be a mom/teacher/cop/baker," and the person said, "Oh, well how are you going to buy a house if you don't make much money?" This happens all the time. Maybe you're even guilty of being that person.

We are told (and we perpetuate) the idea that our careers need to be chosen based on what they provide you: money, status, prestige, etc. We tell ourselves and our children that we follow the money because the money will eventually make us happy. This is social hypnotism and thought control at work.

> ## Dr. Kousouli's Success Secret Tip #8
> ## SUCCESS DOESN'T ALWAYS MEAN MONEY

"Some people are so poor, all they have is money."
~ Patrick Meagher

One of the first questions everyone asks you is, "What do you do for a living?" This automatically sets us up to believe that our defining feature is our job and therefore our paycheck. When re-programming your mind for success, this also means you need to redefine success and move away from traditional beliefs about money and success.

Success can be finding the man or woman of your dreams, living a wonderful life free of worry, having peace of mind, being able to sleep at night, having a child, living to a ripe old age, loving and being loved by a supporting spouse, and attaining the career or education you wanted. Money shouldn't be our only marker of success; the money comes from a long line of other successes, like attaining the career or education you've dreamt of. As we all know, but have a hard time internalizing: "Money doesn't make us happy." We have to focus on what makes us happy; more often than not, the money will follow.

Dr. Kousouli's Success Secret Tip #9
DO IT ALL FOR LOVE, NOT THE MONEY

"I think everyone should get rich and famous and do everything they ever dreamed of so they can see that it's not the answer."
~ Jim Carrey

Many business coaches and self-help gurus ask, "If you could do anything, without considering money or 'success,' what would you do?" This is such a difficult question for us, especially because **we've been brainwashed into believing that what we love to do and what we need to do are two separate things.** But take a moment and really ask yourself that question. If you didn't have to worry about money, what would you choose to do with your life?

As they say, "When you love what you do, you never have to work a day in your life." While there are definitely days that still feel like work, and nothing is ever perfect, you can live the life you love by simply *choosing* to do what you love.

When people ask me what I do, I say I PLAY all day. I couldn't imagine not doing what I love to do, and I want that for you, too. The best part is that I make a living doing what I love - because I had the guts to go out and create based on my gifts. Of course it wasn't easy, and it wasn't overnight. I had to overcome strong opposition and ideas of what I "should" do and "how" I should go about it. I overrode the choices of my guidance counselors, parents, and others to go with what I innately felt was in my own best interest, even though they *thought* they knew best for me.

Why Money Isn't Everything

Yes, we do require money to live in this world. Money is a great thing when used positively, as it allows you more freedom and offers varied life options. This is, however, the *end* benefit of attaining money. If you do everything for the sake of attaining money only, eventually you're going to run out of steam, and there's nothing worse than running out of steam in life because then you become empty. This is why it's so important to refer to the first tip, Build an Unbelievable "Why I Do." Money isn't the end-all-be-all. Money comes after a job well done, and you can't do a job right if you don't love your core reason "why." When you have done the job correctly, the fuel keeps firing the engine; you never run out of steam *and* you earn the money.

Of course, discovering and cultivating your gifts in order to love what you do takes longer than simply running head-first after the money. But what in life is better when it's rushed? Nothing. Take time to cultivate your passion, your love, your inspiration. Take time to do the job right, and the money will eventually follow. Our society has brainwashed us into believing that money equates success. But you know that you don't have to be a sheep anymore, working towards paying bills and consuming just to "survive." Take the steps below to really start living, rather than just chasing a paycheck.

Action Steps for Defining Your Success

1. Take out a pen and paper (yes, again. Writing takes invisible thoughts and translates them into manifested reality on paper, so you can tangibly work with your ideas).

2. Write down a list of things you believe equate to success. Maybe it's money, but make sure you have other things on there, like: "Time with my family. Ability to travel. Being home when my kid starts walking," etc.

3. Ask people who are older than you, especially your grandparents or other elders, how they define success. Ask them what key things matter most in life, and what would they do differently now that they have more wisdom. Make a list of their responses, if you like.

4. Compare your list to the list of those you "interviewed." Strike out anything that doesn't seem like the definition of success. Keep this list, and focus on it whenever you start to wonder if you're truly a success.

5. Focus your time and energy management. Cut out the crap from your day. If you take two hours to do your makeup or get ready for work every morning, you are wasting valuable time that could help you better provide for your success. If you could cut the two hours daily (14 hours weekly), even by half, that gives you 7 hours a week extra. Multiplied by four weeks, that's 28 hours in a month. That's a little bit more than an entire extra day! Multiply that by twelve, and you have twelve days a year in "extra" time – all because you cut out the unnecessary prep time in the morning.

For more valuable tips on how to materialize monetary success through thought, read my other book, *BE A MASTER™ OF PSYCHIC ENERGY.*

Chapter Six:
Don't Work Hard or Smart – Work *Correctly*

"*Work smarter, not harder.*" "*Work hard, play hard.*" How many times have you heard those statements? How many times have you repeated those mantras in your head, assuming that they were going to lead you to success like all those who came before you? I'm here to tell you that working hard and working smarter won't always net you the results you're looking for. You need to work *correctly*.

Don't get me wrong – I am a firm believer in the benefits of working hard for your success. I'm living proof. But what I am saying is that *just* hard work will get you nowhere; millions of people work hard all their lives and end up with nothing in the end. What I have found, through my experiences and the experiences of my clients, is that working *with* the laws of the universe and creation net the best results for everyone.

Dr. Kousouli's Success Secret Tip #10
DO NOT BELIEVE IN LUCK

"I'm a great believer in luck. I find the harder I work,
the more luck I have."
~ *Coleman Cox*

This is what I mean by working correctly. By learning about, understanding, and embracing these laws (like the Law of Attraction), you're arming yourself with every tool needed to manifest your creation in reality. Instead of assigning your and others' success to "dumb luck," you can begin to recognize the forces of energy at work.

31

In our society today, we are often told that we should follow the plans and support the creation that others manifest. We should work for that startup company because, one day, they'll be worth millions, or we should get a steady job with that Big Business because it's always going to be there. We get caught up in the ocean of others' manifestations, rather than focusing on our own.

Once again, this is exactly what our pre-programmed thought control wants from us; to follow the few "shepherds" like sheep so they can keep us under control. They want us to think that success and individuality are a result of spontaneous luck; not connected at all to our ability to harness the powerful laws of the universe, or even utilize our own brains. Think for yourself! **Do not believe in luck. Instead, believe in God, His Laws of the Universe, and YOUR ABILITY to take ACTION!**

Dr. Kousouli's Success Secret Tip #11
NEVER SAY "I'VE MADE IT"

"The man on top of the mountain didn't fall there."
~ *Vince Lombardi*

What's the one thing you want to accomplish in life? Is it having children, traveling to 18 countries, making a billion dollars, or simply living a peaceful life? Goals are amazing things to have and work towards, but goals are made to be achieved. What happens when you achieve those goals? Are you going to sit down and think, "Well that was fun, glad I got that over with!"? Of course not. (If you said yes to that question, you should probably re-evaluate.)

Settling for a few achieved goals makes us stagnate; we begin to decay physically, emotionally, mentally, and spiritually when we stop trying to grow. **We were put on Earth to create – not once or twice, but for our entire lives.** For this reason, I make it a point to never say, "I've made it." This doesn't mean I'm unhappy with where I'm at or that I don't celebrate my successes, it just means that there is no end point in mind; only constant creation.

We've been hypnotized by society to believe that "we've made it" when we retire, when we have had our 1.6 children and a huge house in the suburbs, or when we have built our businesses from the ground up. But what "they" don't tell you is that there is nothing fulfilling about reaching the end. Why are so many people who have the "American Dream" so unhappy? Because these goals are empty when you're not creating something continuously.

Those big TV sets and expensive vacations don't mean anything if you don't have a set of future goals, or a desire to create in mind. We are told to buy, buy, buy, consume, consume, consume – but never create. In the end, it's only constant creation that will leave you feeling whole, happy, and fulfilled. The constant creator is the person that knows you only stop physically creating when you're physically dead. But then you will still create - just in a different way.

Action Steps to Start Working Correctly

1. Take out pen and paper, and your list of "success" definitions.

2. Consider what you do every day that is targeted at your definitions of success. Write down the actions you take that result in "success." Also write down what you spend the majority of your time doing (marketing, administration, browsing the Internet). If what you're doing every day isn't in alignment with what you define as "success," then strike it from the list.

3. Every day, work on doing more of what helps you create that "success" you want, and work to weed out the behaviors or tasks that don't get you where you want to go. I.e. things

like video games, television shows, talking on the phone longer than necessary, smartphone games, and other similar addictions. These are deeply rooted habitual issues that keep you from moving forward.

Pro Tip: To weed out the tasks that don't help you get where you want to go, or that don't make you feel successful, I recommend hiring the experts. For example, if you want to build a house, you may have the raw materials but you most likely have no idea what you're doing. You can work hard all you want, but that house isn't going to look too great.

You can work smarter by using a blueprint. The house might turn out pretty well in some places, but it's going to take you forever to figure out the wiring and plumbing. To work *correctly*, you need to hire an architect, engineers, and the right construction company that knows what they're doing. You save yourself energy and time, and the job gets done right. Hire people whose gifts make up for your shortcomings, or that can do the things that do not honor your creation. Delegate the right challenges to the right people in your team, and don't micromanage everything yourself. This is truly working *correctly*.

Chapter Seven:
Recognize the Divine - In and Around You

Our world is an amazing thing; it is remarkable and complex in ways that humans have only begun to really understand. Even if you're a diehard atheist, you still have to appreciate the wonder that is our reality and our co-existing creation. One of the things that will always, *always* help us root ourselves back in our own reality (rather than in the reality and manifestations of those in control) is to recognize the divine hand in the world around us.

Dr. Kousouli's Success Secret Tip #12
BELIEVE IN A HIGHER POWER

"Believe in yourself and all that you are. Know that there is something inside you that is greater than any obstacle."
~ Christian D. Larson

I understand that not everyone believes as I do, and no two people believe in anything in exactly the same way. But when I say that you should believe in a higher power, I mean that you should recognize there is something more than *you*, more than *us*. Whether you call it *Father God, Jesus Christ, the Holy Spirit, Allah,* etc. Even if you believe that a higher power is just higher wisdom or some innate intuition or higher (superconscious) mind that keeps you breathing and your heart beating, we all recognize an ancient power and divinity in us that we can't deny.

There is something greater than what we experience with our physical senses. If this wasn't the case, why would 92% of all Americans believe in a God or "universal spirit," according to a 2008 Pew

Research Poll? Even 20% of people who defined themselves as athe-ists believed in a higher power of some unknown source. We feel it in our beings, and we constantly seek to understand it. We are continuously looking for the divine, and yet the divine is in all of us. Believing in a divine inner power, we feel as if we can handle any challenge or achieve any desire. **Even though our corporeal body is limited, belief in a higher power helps us know that bigger things are possible.**

Dr. Kousouli's Success Secret Tip #13
DON'T FORGET TO PLAY

"It's a happy talent – to know how to play."
~ Ralph Waldo Emerson

Just because we are creations of God – higher mind, or higher uni-versal power – doesn't mean that we have to bear the weight of the world on our shoulders. You are here to expand as a spiritual being, not to just pay bills, get stressed out, age, and die. Yes, part of our physical work here in this realm takes a little bit of hustle, a little bit of pressure. However, you must align with the joy in the world also, which exists and awaits your focused attention. Cre-ation works best when we're in a childlike energy state, and when we are full of bliss.

We were created to create; don't ever forget that. When we cre-ate, our divine energy is relaxed, it's free-flowing, and it allows us to truly recognize the divine in others and ourselves. Why else do you feel so accomplished, happy, and free after you've done something you love, such as singing a song, drawing a picture, building some-thing, or enjoying a relaxing day with family and friends? The joy in our lives deserves divine recognition, so don't neglect it. Laugh and play – loudly – and don't be boring.

Dr. Kousouli's Success Secret Tip #14
KNOW YOU ARE DIVINE, BUT CHECK THE EGO

"I searched for God and found only myself. I searched
for myself and found only God."
~ Sufi Proverb

You are a servant of the Universe. Whatever god, entity, energy, or power you acknowledge in this realm of existence, you know you are a divining rod – a channel for the power – but not the only 'Source' itself. As you rise in worldly power and prestige, you may find yourself feeling especially blessed or powerful - but do not assume that the Laws of the Universe work only for you. Do not get cocky; do not expect the universe to unfold only at your feet. You are a creator amongst creators made by the 'Creator'; a part of this magnificent world we live in, but you are not the One Creator or Source. Many are the leaders who rose and fell fast because of an ego that was way out of control.

It's also important to know that once you've embraced your divine energy, and embraced the Laws of the Universe as powerful tools in your success, others may begin to project their insecurities on to you. Understand that you must not let it get to you. As we spoke about before, negative energy seeks positive energy to help it balance itself out. Do not give your energy to these people, thoughts, or social norms. You are divine, and you work with the universe to create boundlessly.

Dr. Kousouli's Success Secret Tip #15
DIVINE GROWTH IS WHAT IT'S ALL ABOUT

"We grow when we win, we grow when we fail. No matter
what we do, we can't stop divine growth."
~ Dr. Theo Kousouli

People don't take enough time to go past the five senses. Look into your spirituality; evaluate the different spiritual systems available. Don't settle until you've seen what each one has to offer. Look at the original roots of early Christianity if you're going to be a Christian. Don't get caught up in fanaticism, but learn from everyone. Find something that vibrates with you and your heart – no matter what others think. When you spiritually grow, your business and personal life will grow as well – it's a divine connection. You'll be surprised that when you work to flow abundance to others, divine energy will flow through you to make it easier. For a deeper understanding of this and to learn about how you can harness your energy to improve your life and the life of those around you, check out my book, *BE A MASTER™ OF PSYCHIC ENERGY.*

Action Steps to Discovering the Divine

1. Attend services in a new church, synagogue, temple, or any other house of worship. See what you have to learn, feel the energy, and learn something new. Do not take your judgment with you. Go with an open heart and mind; see how others are led to their understanding of God. Remember that everyone is hypnotized into a "box" of belief from youth.

2. Try any number of spiritual activities, like deep meditation and prayer while listening to Byzantine or Gregorian music. Focus on visualization and your dreams. Connect with a trusted, God-centered spiritual guide who can safely connect you to a better understanding of the spiritual realm. Explore every area that you can think of, and see what you learn.

3. Seek out alternative and spiritual health healers; energy healers, light healers, DMT shamans, priests, etc., who work with the light of God. These people are like divining rods, full

of energy from the Source that they can share with you; just be sure you fully screen who you allow to lead you in spiritual matters. Not all who say they are "of the light" - are of the correct 'light.'

4. Keep doing what feels right to your soul, and find ways to implement what you learn in your everyday business life. Business is very spiritually rooted – remember that. In business, you seek to serve others by giving of your skills and what you know in order to manifest your sustenance.

Chapter Eight:
Know Thyself - Inside and Out

As mentioned throughout this book, our purpose on Earth is to create, just as the Creator created us. But what if you're reading this and thinking, "What is my gift, and what can I possibly create?" That's an incredibly difficult place to be in, but there are plenty of ways to find yourself and your gift, and start working with the universe to fully realize your potential in order to start creating.

Once you fully grasp your personality, understand your talents, and have a direction, you're limitless. But first, you have to understand all that!

Dr. Kousouli's Success Secret Tip #16
YOU WILL NEVER GO WRONG INVESTING IN YOURSELF

"Investing in yourself is the best investment you will ever make.
It will not only improve your life, it will improve the lives
of all those around you."
~ Robin S. Sharma

So often in life we have a hard time prioritizing ourselves, especially if we work in a care capacity, have children, or have other people relying on us. Spending money on ourselves or taking time to care for ourselves seems totally selfish and like a waste of resources. You think, "But I could do so much/help so many people/give someone else something with that time/money/effort."

When we stop putting ourselves and our creation first, we stagnate. As you know, that's an insult to our Creator and our divine selves. For this reason, I highly recommend that you get over the hurdles that are preventing you from investing in yourself. Self-help books, seminars, healing therapies, education, new skill training, and even a trip to the spa to treat yourself – all of these things can help you learn to create, create better, and prevent you from decay and inaction. That money, time, and/or effort you place into these self-improvement activities will be returned to you tenfold in whichever way you choose to create.

Maybe you want to learn how to paint, and can start painting even more amazing works of art after a class. Maybe you're a doctor, and want to learn how to provide more for your patients by taking an alternative medicine course. Whatever it is, the energy you put into yourself will be returned by the Universe in the form of your creation.

Dr. Kousouli's Success Secret Tip #17
IMPROVE EVERY DAY IN SOME TINY WAY

"The secret of change is to focus all of your energy, not on fighting the old, but on building the new."

~ Socrates

Much like we need to invest in ourselves in order to understand ourselves fully, we also need to challenge ourselves daily to see what we are truly capable of. This may mean taking a course, learning a new skill, reading an educational book, or watching a documentary.

For others it may mean a 30-day exercise challenge, or trying a new recipe with food you've never cooked. Maybe it means finally seeking therapy for your troubled relationship, or turning off the TV and going for a walk instead. When we tell ourselves, "I want to change *this*," we are growing in all aspects of ourselves – emotionally, mentally, physically, and spiritually.

By setting small daily, weekly, or monthly goals for ourselves and expecting to see change in that allotted time frame, we're giving ourselves small wins that help us keep improving. More importantly, expecting more of yourself each and every day shows *you* just what you're made of, and it makes it easier for you to understand just what separates you from the pack.

Dr. Kousouli's Success Secret Tip #18
FULLY KNOW THYSELF

"Knowing yourself is the beginning of all wisdom."
~ Aristotle

Use every chance you can to get information about who you are. Learn about yourself. Study yourself. There are so many tools in this modern era, and they're as simple as personality tests or reading about psychology, and can be as advanced as regression hypnotherapy, spiritual retreats, and the careful use of psychedelic herbs by qualified doctors or experts in the field of multidimensional awareness.

Of course, not every option that other people have used to "find themselves" is appropriate for you; that's part of the process. Many people prefer strengthening their religious connections (churches, synagogues, temples, etc.), meditation, journaling, and even counseling to help understand themselves a little bit better before diving into the really deep stuff. If you've had an especially traumatic past, regression hypnotherapy could really make a world of difference in helping you sort through what happened in the past, and understand how it is still troubling you in the present.

Don't ever underestimate the tools you come across to help you in your self-discovery. The best part about growing and changing is that we will constantly surprise ourselves, so never stop trying to learn more about who you are and what you're capable of. **Read BE A MASTER™ OF SELF LOVE for more information on truly loving yourself.**

Action Steps to Know Thyself

1. Spend time alone. Yes, alone. Do not couch surf, do not browse the Internet, do not read. Spend time quietly with yourself, and think about what you know about yourself, what you wish you understood better, what you want to change, etc. Don't write anything down. Just learn how to be with yourself, and how to face yourself.

2. Get away from the noise of others. I recommend meditating in a park or garden, getting away from the city, asking for quiet time away from your family, etc. Spend this time thinking about your goals, your desires, what makes you tick, etc. You can't know yourself fully if you always have other people's thought energy and input in your head.

3. Invest in books, seminars, courses, clubs, camps, groups, etc. that will help you develop skills or talents you want to grow. Find a way to commit time and energy to growth, and don't feel guilty about it. You deserve it!

Chapter Nine:
Create a Loving, Winning Lifestyle

A s we just discussed, there is only one you and you must choose to live your life the way (or ways) that honor your creation. But in our lives, we are so hardwired to live a certain way, even in our most private lives, that sometimes it's hard to break free and live the life we really want to live. In order to truly reprogram yourself and accept a life of success and happiness (as you define those terms), you need to shed a bright light on every aspect of your life, including everything from romance to relationships.

Dr. Kousouli's Success Secret Tip #19
BE SINGLE; LOVE YOU

"Don't be scared to walk alone. Don't be scared to like it."

~ John Mayer

Do you remember teasing other kids (or getting teased by other kids) with the "Love and Marriage" song? "Bobby and Jane, sitting in a tree, K-I-S-S-I-N-G. First comes love, then comes marriage, then comes baby in the baby carriage!" Despite railing against this assigned lifestyle as a little kid ("I'm never getting married!"), the majority of us fall in line by our early adult years. By the age of 25, almost 80% of Americans will be married *for the first time*. The average age of a first divorce is 30 years old, with the average marriage lasting about 8 years. Pew Research also found, in their 2014 poll on marriage in the United States, that people only wait about 3 years to get remarried, and that second marriages are twice as likely to end in divorce as well.

But the most shocking statistic, in my opinion, is that by 25 years old **only 16% of people are unmarried.** The majority of that 16%, the same Pew Research study says, have significant others or life partners living with them. And yet, we often split from these people before we're 30, marriage certificate or not. And we fall back into committed relationships within just a few short years. And so I ask you: **How do you know who you want to spend your life with if you haven't even spent time getting to know *you*?**

Our society has drilled it into us that we have to find a mate, that we have to build a relationship, a home, a family with someone else. All the while we don't ever stop and ask: Why? We're perfectly functional on our own, and some of us even operate better with a modicum of solitude. This isn't just the U.S.; this is a phenomenon we see all over the globe. In some places, like China, women who aren't married by 27 are publicly called "leftovers," and parents begin to panic and seek matchmakers for their children.

What does this tell us? It tells us we aren't good enough on our own. It tells us that in order to live a fulfilling life, we have to pair up and work towards the same thing everyone else is. *This is thought control at work.* If you're currently in a relationship, I'm not saying to hurry up and end it so you can grow as a person. I'm saying: **If you are single right now, embrace it. Do not rush into something just because everyone tells you to. And for heaven's sake, don't get into a relationship just because you're lonely or bored!**

Everyone should fully learn about themselves through their twenties and early thirties, taking the time to truly know what they expect of themselves, their talents, and the people around them. Remember: you are a divine creation. Why would you want to settle for a relationship that doesn't honor that and is of the same nature? A true love relationship will support you and your creations, rather than distract you into following the crowd. Your cup can't runneth over enough to fill up another's cup until you have something solid that fills up your cup. You can't break your path for the sake of someone else's happiness. When you are ready, you will find someone who is traveling down their own similar path, and you may then choose to continue on a journey together. This would truly be a match made in heaven.

Dr. Kousouli's Success Secret Tip #20
BURN NO BRIDGES; BARRICADE SOME

"Never cut what you can untie."
~ Robert Frost

Burning bridges means that you cut all ties (and never talk to or see someone ever again), usually in a dramatic and fairly negative fashion. Think about that time you quit the job you hated, and instead of putting in your two weeks notice, you just walked out. Or when you broke up with your significant other in a very loud, screaming way and said, "I never want to see you again!" While these definitely feel wonderful in the moment because you're letting off steam, they lower our vibrational energy and reflect negatively in our lives later. Essentially, you're giving too much of your personal energy to their negative energy. And if you don't deal with the situation correctly, it does come back to bite you in the rear later.

This is why I tell people to never burn bridges, but barricade them if needed. Some people are so toxic, they infect others with their insensitivity, laziness, bad character, morals, and work ethic, and they usually show no clear positive direction. Many times these people are very jealous of anyone who excels and does well in life. They secretly wish even their close friends and relatives harm or failure, due to their own low self-esteem and lack of confidence in their abilities. These energy vampires need to be blocked out of your life so they don't drain you, but you also don't want to give them a burst of your energy by investing in the process (by burning the bridge completely in a negative fashion).

You can retain your dignity and your positive energy by simply day-by-day, week-by-week removing these people or situations from your life. Give them less of your time and energy until they completely fade away. Also, if you have been very mature in your handling of the breakup, you have the option to un-barricade the connection later, if circumstances and opportunity provide a win-win situation for you both. But if you're feeling overwhelmed and weighed down by the person's continued bombardment of negativity, remember that you are a creation of the Divine, and energy vampires cannot have a place in the light – so don't give it to them. You will find that you will skyrocket in success much quicker without all the dead weight.

Dr. Kousouli's Success Secret Tip #21
BE ALLERGIC TO LOSERS; MAGNETIZED TO WINNERS

"Surround yourself with people who will only lift you higher. Life is full of people who want to bring you down."
~ Carlina Davidson

Have you ever met a person who just seems to have their stuff together, and who is surrounded by the same types of people? Inversely, have you noticed that negative people tend to attract other equally negative people? "Misery loves company" and all that. This isn't just a result of random chance, but rather a manifestation of the true Laws of the Universe. As we've talked about in previous chapters, negative energy seeks positive energy in order to gain more for itself. Negative energy only seeks to attach itself to other energy to infect and take over, not create on its own! But when positive energy seeks positive energy, the bond and stability they create is unrivaled.

Another reason to only seek people who have their life together? Studies have actually found that people with poor habits or health issues actually create those same habits and health issues in their closest companions. In a study done at the University of California, San Diego in 2009, researchers found that - out of a social network of 2,200 students – the ones with the highest grades clumped together, the ones who were unfit and heavily out of shape were closest friends, and so on. "Like attracts like," and in this instance, you have the power to control your "Like."

On a fundamental level, this tells us that focusing on your energy and what you put out into the world will come back to you in the form of friends, alliances, teammates, and a network of people who think and feel just like you. You'll become an integral part of a team of winners, rather than being the only winner getting your energy sucked dry by energy vampires. Remember that who your friends are and who you hang around with is the sum total of who you become. Look around at the people that surround you: are they energy vampires, or are they like the sun's solar power, recharging you and allowing you to work better than ever before? Also remember that time (not money) is the only real gold currency we have while we are living; don't let anyone or anything waste your time.

Action Steps for Creating a Winning Lifestyle

1. Find one thing you want to learn how to do and invest in learning how to do it. This could be something like learning how to cook, or learning a new software program, or taking a college course towards a new degree. Pick something that is in alignment with what you consider "success," but it doesn't matter what area of life it pertains to (business, relationships, self, etc.).

2. Make a list of people who build you up, and a list of people

who drain you. Mentally dismiss the people on the draining side of the list, and reach out to the people who build you up and ask to "hang out," meet up, etc. Spend more time with the positive people.

3. Be self-aware. Changing your lifestyle and the people around you takes time, and can be challenging as you go down the path a little ways. Constantly take stock of how something makes you feel as a person; your energy will let you know when something is beneficial, and when something is dragging you down.

Chapter Ten:
The Power of Collaboration

Most of this book has been devoted to focusing on *you* and what you have to contribute to the world. In this chapter, though, we're going to talk about just how important it is to find those powerfully positive people in your life and your career. Without people who challenge you, support you, and encourage you to do more and be better, we stagnate. It's impossible to go anywhere in this world without a helping hand from another, and you can't say that you've reached any level of success if you climb to the top of the mountain and have no one to share the view with.

Dr. Kousouli's Success Secret Tip #22
ALLIANCES ARE ESSENTIAL FOR THRIVING

"As iron sharpens iron, so one friend sharpens another."
~ Proverbs 27:17

In our not-so-long ago past, humans only survived when they formed alliances. Our ancestors learned to travel together to increase odds of survival. Now, we're not exactly living in caves and scavenging for berries, but that doesn't mean we don't need other humans. In fact, the exact opposite is true. How many times have you heard, "It's not *what* you know, it's *who* you know and who knows you"? If you're an entrepreneur or have ever held a job period, you know this statement is 100% true. It's pretty much always been true. We tend to attract and associate with those we like, respect, and admire.

To truly form alliances that will change your life, though, you can't just pick people because of what they can offer you. Choose people to be in your circle because they have a variety of goals, be-haviors, and desires – but most of all, pick them because they make you better. Join a networking group and build alliances with those in similar as well as different markets.

Dr. Kousouli's Success Secret Tip #23
JOIN OR CREATE A WEEKLY GROUP THINK TANK

"A small group of determined and like-minded people can change the course of history."
~ Mahatma Gandhi

Think of a big corporate office. What do you see the most (aside from energy-sucking cubicles)? Board rooms and conference spaces! Tons of them! Why? Because convening and interacting with others in your field and outside of it is one of the most powerful ways to get the creative and productive juices flowing. Even big corporations that are part of the thought control and sheep-herding cycle know the importance of weekly group think tanks and meet-ups.

When you're set on breaking away from the herd and creating success for yourself, what better way to do this than to actually interact with people who inspire you and help you create more and better? By taking the step to surround yourself with like-minded and passionate people, you're taking that first step to tell the universe, "I am manifesting my desires." This also relates back to working correctly; if you have a team around you, you don't have to do it all yourself. Hire or form alliances with people who are experts in their field, and benefit from the easy manifestations of your creations.

Once you start group think tanks or create a group of "board members" to help you review and process your ideas, you will have tapped into the power that helps you succeed in life and business. From there, the universe will meet you halfway and help you to manifest everything you've ever wanted. But first, you have to take the time to seek out people who will help you put in the work. I teach the concept of group manifestation much more in depth in BE A MASTER™ OF PSYCHIC ENERGY.

Dr. Kousouli's Success Secret Tip #24
NETWORKING MEANS GROWING

"The currency of real networking is not greed but generosity."
~ *Keith Ferrazzi*

I want you to immediately forget the idea of "work networking" – only making connections fast and easy so you can build up connections that benefit you. Instead, replace it with "making honey."

Making Honey

What do networking and growing have in common? Both are uncomfortable and most people hate the effort required to do both. But if you change the way you perceive networking and growth, you will find it easier to get through them both. One meeting with a new person or several people can yield you new clients or new friends. Immediate expansion of your world occurs.

Think of a bee and how - if it didn't network between the hive, queen bee and flowers - you wouldn't have delicious honey. Your honey is the fruits of your labor, which is often reflective of the amount of networking you have done! Also note that the queen bee doesn't do all the work herself; she delegates to the worker bees that make her honey yield much higher. Invest in other people and their expertise – you will make much more "honey" this way!

How much networking you've done often shows up as how much money or "honey" you have (given by your fellow man because you're supplying a product or services). Isn't that interesting?

You can't make honey staying in the hive. You got to get excited and go out there; be of service first to others, offer your services, meet new people, buzz around, and have fun!

Action Steps for Collaborating With Others

1. Ask people at work or in your wider network if they'd like to meet outside of work or during your off time to discuss and share ideas. Explain the think tank and that you're hoping to find like-minded individuals. People will be excited by the idea!

2. Take a notebook with you wherever you are. When someone gives you a golden nugget of information or wisdom, write it down immediately. Take your notebook to your group think tanks and let wisdom fall onto your pages!

3. If you have attended any one of my seminars on how to use your energy in a group scenario to attract more success, you may already be participating in the personalized group events. Look into networking sites such as Mark E. Sackett's 'TheArtofActiveNetworking' or 'Meetup' and see if you can find groups who support your passions or goals. Also expand your knowledge of marketing your brand by connecting with speakers like Bob Proctor, James Malinchak and Craig Duswalt. There are plenty of entrepreneurs, artists, masterminds, and other meet-up groups that meet weekly in every city. Create one if you can't find one.

4. Don't be afraid to follow up and contact people first. Other people are just as afraid of reaching out as you are. Ask for advice, pitch ideas, and just reach out to make a connection without expecting anything in return. This is how you make "honey." People like to do business with those they are familiar

with, which means by the third or fourth contact someone is generally ready to try out your service. Remember: "The success of the come-up is in the follow-up"!

5. USE SOCIAL MEDIA. Join groups on social media, follow/ like figures you admire or want to connect with, and engage with their content, posts, and fan base, which can help you with ideas for your business.

6. Leverage all your talents and connections. If you don't have much capital but lots of skill and talent, find the people or companies who need your skill and talent. Trade your resources for capital by being hired and paid for helping them achieve their goals. This can take some time at the beginning and definitely much dedication and drive to see the saving and investing process through. Don't despair; keep moving forward to get the needed monies in order to take your next calculated step of growth. If you already have capital and want to get a job done but don't have the skill or talent, stretch your money and hire the best people with the skill-set and talent you are missing to get your goal(s) accomplished. The more you connect yourself to others' resources and leverage both your talents and connections, the faster your success in will come.

Chapter Eleven:
Above and Beyond in Business

Before you become successful in whichever way *you* define success, you need to become confident in yourself and your ways. Master your skills, your trade, and your passion. Make it better, make it yours, and make your mark on the path that you're on. Become your message, and spread that message. Teach others with love, understanding, and compassion; don't annoy them with your message. *Give it to them* with love. Teach and show by example instead of yelling and screaming from your soapbox.

When you provide a service, product, message, or brand to people, let it be a reflection of you and your personality, as well as your desire to make a difference, rather than just pumping it out to make money. That is not sustainable, and people will be able to innately tell the difference. You must genuinely care about the person and their needs first and foremost.

Dr. Kousouli's Success Secret Tip #25
MARKET YOUR PASSION AS IF YOUR LIFE DEPENDED ON IT

"Meet people then stay in touch with them forever. You just never know where it could lead."
~ James Malinchak

In order to properly market yourself, your product, or your ideas, you have to instead focus on marketing your passion. While marketing your product will get the mass public to fall in love with your product, the people who will keep your brand, product, service, or message going are the people who can think for themselves and want to continue to grow. You want to help these higher-level people succeed even more with your service or product. The traditional customer doesn't know what he or she needs; use your expertise to show them what you can offer. Show them your passion for what you're providing, and show them how it reflects their needs and provides them value. Then, and only then, will your marketing work correctly for you – and them. Always look to create a win-win situation for all parties involved.

Shotgunner vs. Precision Sniper

There is a difference between a shotgun and a single bullet placed well. Shotguns pepper the area with small holes, hoping to hit a target, while single caliber guns shoot straight and have a much more impactful effect when they meet their mark. Don't shotgun the market, target your audience and aim for that market. Your customers will be able to tell the difference; they will pay for something that is specifically targeted for them and something that you're passionate about.

Customers respond the best to products of value, rather than products for profit. Don't sell; instead, invest in value systems. Laser-focus on how your product helps another human being or solves a problem for someone. Appeal to that, and show your passion for providing value.

Dr. Kousouli's Success Secret Tip #26
BELIEVE IN DELIVERING QUALITY, NOT JUST QUANTITY

"Strive not to be a success, but rather of value."
~ Albert Einstein

Think of a company that you align with quality. Is it a car brand? An electronics brand? A service company? Think about how much more you're willing to pay for their services because of the *quality* they provide, rather than the speed or high volumes. You want to emulate these companies and these people. No matter your product, service, or message, make your name or your brand synonymous with quality.

When someone comes to me for health care or to learn how to master their mind, I believe that every single person deserves my quality work. People will always remember the quality you provided.

Dr. Kousouli's Success Secret Tip #27
PUT YOUR NAME WITH PRIDE INTO YOUR WORK;
IT'S YOUR SIGNATURE

"Go the extra mile – it's never crowded."
~ Wayne Dyer

I feel like I've done a job well when I sign 'KOUSOULI' on a service or product. I don't want anything to have my signature that isn't inherently purposeful or of the highest quality. No matter what your work is, whether a work of art, a new product, a new idea – make it yours and make sure that it's so good you *want* to put your name on it. People who churn out products and services without any desire to put their name on it are not providing a quality product; they're providing quantity.

Just like you want to provide value, you want to keep your name synonymous with value and quality. When people see your name on something, you want them to buy it because they know it's going to be good. Put the right energy into the product or service, and that energy will come back to you. Energy out is energy in - remember that.

Action Steps to Go Above and Beyond

1. Spend a lot of time thinking about your product, service, or message. Think back to your "Why I Do" list, and consider new ventures in business to see if they align with your true values. Your customers will be able to tell the difference.

2. Really take time to understand your clients and market. If you don't understand them, they won't understand you.

3. Learn from the people who aren't afraid to put their signature on everything that they create in quality. Study them and their brand. Understand what it means to really own your own brand, your signature, and always put out quality you can be proud of.

Chapter Twelve:
When It All Hits the Fan

So you've spent some time truly evaluating your life, the influencers that control your thoughts, and you've decided on a path or direction you want to go. Maybe you're already feeling motivated, maybe you've already begun to create like only *you* can. You've invoked the Laws of the Universe, and you're growing and expanding in new ways every day. You've done it. You've hypnotized yourself for success.

But you're not done – you know it. You know nothing is ever "this easy," right? (Not that this has been easy.) There will still be road bumps, there will still be days where you think, "I just can't do this." There are people who own multimillion-dollar companies, who have done what they've always dreamt of doing, and who feel like they really have their stuff together, and they still encounter stormy seas.

So how do you keep yourself on positive autopilot when it all seems like it's hitting the proverbial fan? Keep on sailing. Use the tips below to help reset your compass, and keep exploring and creating.

Dr. Kousouli's Success Secret Tip #28
TURN ALL FAILURES INTO WINS

"Failure is the opportunity to begin again more intelligently."
~ Henry Ford

No matter how bad you think you've failed, I can promise you one thing: you learned something crucial. Whether you've failed a test, crashed your car, broke up with your life partner, lost a business, foreclosed on a house, fought with your child - whatever happened is a learning experience. Instead of beating yourself up over what you didn't do, take a step back and evaluate the steps that led to this moment.

Ask yourself: "Where did I misstep? Why did I think that was the best step?" And most importantly, "What can I do to avoid this next time?" Just like a child has to learn from experience that a stove is hot, or they shouldn't run by the side of the pool, we all have to learn from our mistakes. We *will* make mistakes. It's part of our learning process; you can't know yourself or the world around you fully without "failing" in some way. The biggest failure of all is failing to make mistakes, though, because it means you're not growing.

Next time you feel like you're just a walking failure, take a deep breath and tell yourself: "I'll live through it, I'll learn from it, and I'll grow from it." And then keep creating.

Dr. Kousouli's Success Secret Tip #29
USE FEAR TO MOTIVATE YOURSELF INTO MORE POWER

"A ship is always safe in harbor, but that's not what ships are for."
~ William Shedd

Fear is one of our most basic instincts, and it doesn't take much to flare it up. This is why social hypnosis and thought control works so well on humans; our fear response is triggered by almost anything. But what we're not told by those in power is that fear is just as capable of causing a positive reaction as it at making us withdraw. You've heard of "Fight or Flight" responses from adrenaline; it's a biochemical reaction to external stimuli or even perceived threats.

This is what is going to separate you from the sheep. Instead of choosing *flight*, you're going to choose to *fight*. Next time you fail, next time you're scared out of your pants, next time you don't know which way to go - you're going to take a step forward rather than taking two steps back. Using our fear to force us into submission is something that the "authorities" of the world have been doing as long as they've been in power. "You can't do that, there's too much to lose if you fail," or, "There's so much in the world that you don't know – you better stay where it's safe." These are scare tactics, but you have seen behind the curtain now.

Instead of backing down from a challenge or avoiding discomfort, you're going to walk right through it. The people that choose to keep moving when they're afraid are the people who succeed, the people who create the most in this world. If you let your pre-programming think for you, you'll always be hiding. Stop hiding; start living. You're worth it!

Dr. Kousouli's Success Secret Tip #30
YOUR MISTAKES TODAY ARE YOUR STEPS TO GREATNESS TOMORROW

"Although now successful, when I reflect on past failures, I am grateful for the ones to come."
~ Dr. Theo Kousouli

Do you think that everyone who has made something of themselves succeeded on the first try? I sure hope not, because that couldn't be further from the truth. Consider major scientific breakthroughs, like Thomas Edison's creation of the light bulb, how many times Henry Ford tried to create a motor vehicle, how many publishers turned down JK Rowling. And even though they failed so much, they still changed the world.

When you fail, it means you've learned that one particular path doesn't get where you want to go. Forge a new path; turn around and find the fork in the road and take the other path. You're never stuck when you fail; it's not the end of the road, it's just the end of this particular path. Failure can bring greatness if you don't give up; just push past it. Don't let failure define you. You define what was or was not a failure.

> ## Dr. Kousouli's Success Secret Tip #31
> ## COMMIT TO YOUR GREATNESS

"Most people fail, not because of lack of desire, but because of lack of commitment."
~ Vince Lombardi

After reading this book, I hope you've come to the conclusion that you are capable of amazing things. I hope you know that you've only got to harness the innate power within you in order to make even more amazing things happen. But most of all, I hope that this isn't a passing fancy. I hope this is a life-changing, mind-blowing, paradigm-shifting challenge for you. And I hope you commit to it. Every. single. day.

If you don't commit to your greatness, you're not fully harnessing your power. Apathy has to be one of the most overlooked sins; if you're not all in, you're all out. You must commit to your greatness because there are people that are counting on you. To become a leader, you must lead. Leaders don't accept low-level vibrations; they seek higher-level achievements and expect that of themselves on a daily basis.

Action Steps for Thriving Through Failure

1. Think about all the times you've failed, and how many times you've bounced back. Go as far back as when you learned to ride a bicycle. You fell a lot every day, but there came a point you didn't scrape your knees anymore and rejoiced with a

smile as you rode into the wind. Remember that failure does not break you; it makes you stronger.

2. Fail intentionally, just to prove to yourself that you'll still survive. Try to do something you know you're not great at, like skiing or writing code for a website. Pitch a client or idea without knowing the outcome. Ask a beautiful woman or man out on a date. Be in a state of fun and joy; laugh out loud even if it doesn't turn out well. Have no expectations, just put yourself out there. Get uncomfortable, and get used to being uncomfortable. You never grow in your comfort zone.

3. Revisit your "Why I Do" list or your list of what success looks like to you when you're feeling like giving up. Jogging your memory can help you get back up on that horse again, and give you the power to blast through a road block.

4. Recall your spiritual supports. Meditate, pray, visit your place of worship. Whatever you decided was your spiritual fuel, it's time to fill up again. Recalling your divine nature and asking for help from the Higher Source will help you put things into perspective. You may have failed this one, but you are still a product of the Creator, and you're still here to create.

Chapter Thirteen:
Focus on the Journey, Not the Destination

Ask anyone who has reached the end of their career, or even their life, what they wish they would have done if they could do it over again. Odds are, you'll hear some variation of: "I wish I had worried less," or, "I wish I had spent more time with my family," or, "I wish I had taken more chances instead of staying stuck in the same spot." Obviously, hindsight is always 20/20.

What I hope this book does for you is provide some "premature hindsight" – a way to look at your life now and let you know that *this isn't how it has to be forever*. But the other message I want to pass on to you is that you can't rush things; you have to work correctly, you have to persevere, and you have to cultivate your creation. This is not an overnight success, and who wants an overnight success? The longer you spend creating your life and your passion, the longer lived it (and you) will be. Most importantly, you will be moving forward in joy and bliss.

Dr. Kousouli's Success Secret Tip #32
BE FLEXIBLE AS YOU MOVE TOWARDS YOUR VISION OF THE FUTURE

"Blessed are the flexible, for they shall not be bent out of shape."
~ Michael McGriffy

I hope one of the major lessons you take away from this book is that there isn't just *one* way to do something, despite what we've been taught. You are unique, and so are your talents and creations. This means that the ways you approach problems and goals are entirely different from how I or anyone else will approach them – and that's a good thing! Remember; everyone is making it all up as they go along! We're all figuring it out as we live our lives one day at a time - the best we can.

It also means that you can't hold your goals in stone without being open to all possibilities. Trust that you will reach your goals, you will find what you are looking for – the universe *wants* you to get there and will support you every step of the way. But when you want to take only one particular path, you're shutting yourself off to a plethora of enriching and amazing experiences that can influence your future just as much as your goal. Be flexible; take different paths, decide you want to turn back and go another way. It's your life, it's your map, it's your journey. You'll get there (wherever *there* is for you) eventually, and then you'll plot a new course and get somewhere else. It's a never-ending adventure! Enjoy it all!

Dr. Kousouli's Success Secret Tip #33
PUT GOD FIRST AND LET THIS BE YOUR ROCKET FUEL

"Not being excited is to have missed the whole point of life."
~ Steve Chandler

Everything you accomplish is by the grace of God; remember that. And when you put God first you will indeed succeed. This should get you very excited, because once you understand that the true power for success comes from a power larger than you, you will know that you have this energy with you 24/7. When you are surrounded by this energy, what can harm you? Nothing! Who should you fear? No one! Thus, your confidence naturally skyrockets. So does your excitement for life!

What does excitement mean? To excite is to spark, to rouse to action. Your passion will give you something to work towards, but raw excitement and belief in the power of God will keep you going even when the going gets tough. Multiple studies in different areas of psychology have found that the people who are *excited* about their goals are much more likely to achieve them, compared to people who are just working towards the goals because "they should."

You're past the point of doing things just because you *should*, because it's "just what you should do." It's time to go from sheep to shepherd. That's what you've worked through in this book - breaking your pre-programming to truly realize the greater "You" inside. Let the new knowledge you've gained here wash over you, put God first, and let the excitement for your life take over!

Action Steps to Starting on Your Journey

1. Put God first. Meditate, pray, envision your goal and mark it down.

2. Put it on the calendar - whatever *it* is. Get excited about the countdown.

3. Tell friends who can remind you of your upcoming goals and let them get excited with you.

4. Have a healthy yet simple reward waiting for you (i.e. organic sulfite-free wine and probiotic chocolates or a day at the spa) when you reach a certain milestone.

5. Celebrate achievements - small steps deserve attention, too.

Chapter Fourteen:
Conclusion

"You are the master of your destiny. You can influence, direct and control your own environment. You can make your life what you want it to be."

~ *Napoleon Hill*

As you finish this book, I sincerely hope you're about to jump out of your seat with excitement! I hope this book infuses you with the power, knowledge, and inspiration you need to forge ahead. Most of all, I hope you have the bravery to be *excited*. So often in this world, we don't hold our head up or get our hopes up because we don't want everyone else to see us fail, or because we feel we'll let someone down. We've been told our whole lives that it's much less embarrassing to never try than it is to fail. But this is a lie.

Think of anyone in this world that has done anything great, incredible, or unbelievable even. Man has built skyscrapers as high as the eye can see, he's climbed the tallest mountains, dove to the deepest seas, and has even flown through space and landed on the moon! Someone just like you did those things. Someone human just like you, who at one point had doubts and fears – and was told they couldn't do it.

But just like you, they chose to blast through their limiting beliefs and believe in the divine power that resides within. Just like you, they chose to take the lead in their life and no longer rely on loser excuses. Just like you, they didn't listen to the naysayers and lower-level minds. Just like you, they chose to be their own mind-master instead of a mind-slave; they took a stand to make their life as outstanding and as amazing as it should be.

I did it... and yes, so can you!

See you at the seminars!

In the highest vibration of love and light - God bless,

Theodoros Kousouli D.C., CHt.

About the Author

A holistic health care advisor, teacher, speaker, mentor and author who is featured on major networks, Theodoros Kousouli D.C., CHt., is Los Angeles' premier holistic metaphysical energy healer. He is recognized and trusted for effective, quick, drug-free results. His remarkable natural, pain-free, holistic healing system - the Kousouli® Method - focuses on getting patients to their top performance levels by unblocking pathways using the body's own repair mechanisms.

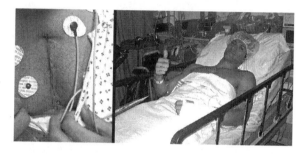

His desire to help others stems from his personal journey recovering from semi-paralysis and major heart surgery, and includes everything he's learned about the optimum wellness techniques that define his practice.

Dr. Theo Kousouli is the author of *five previous books*, including: *BE A MASTER™ of PSYCHIC ENERGY and BE A MASTER™ of MAXIMUM HEALING*. A personal coach and advisor to entertainers, business leaders, energy healers, and spiritual seekers of all varieties, Dr. Kousouli holds seminars teaching people how to tap into their inner healing and higher-level abilities through the use of their nervous systems. Visit **www.KousouliMethod.com** for more information on developing your intuition and personal power to live a more purpose-filled, meaningful, and healthy life. Dr. Kousouli is the ideal speaker for your next event.

To Schedule Dr. Theo Kousouli To Speak At Your Event:
www.DrKousouli.com